James & Marcela, with very warm thanks for all your support, and even warmer congratulations on your wedding!

BEMUSED BY SO MUCH RAIN

Poems by Juliet Gowan

Juliet Gowan

STAMP Publishing

First published 2003
by Stamp Publishing
101 Turnmill Street, Farringdon, London EC1M 5QP

© 2003 Juliet Gowan

Typeset in Monotype Bembo by Richard Cook

Printed and bound in Great Britain by Talisman, Rainham

British Library Cataloguing in Publication Data
A catalogue record for this book is available from the British Library

ISBN 0-9544879-0-7

To my sister, 'Button' (Cecilia Bingham)
and to my mother, Margaret Gowan.
People talk of belief, and I think of these two.

CONTENTS

FOREWORD

When the Present has latched its postern behind my
tremulous stay
And the May month flaps its glad green leaves
like wings,
Delicate-filmed as new-spun silk,
will the neighbours say
"He was a man who used to notice such things"?

From *Afterwards* by Thomas Hardy

M any people will have experience of those numinous
moments of perception hinted at by Hardy. They often
come at unexpected or seemingly incongruous times, and a new
understanding of life seems to flood the soul. But for many of us
to describe these moments is an impossible task. Adequate
language is wanting and the emotional heights and depths of
experience must remain uncommunicated.

But the poet knows better. He does not try to rise above
habitual, bread-and-butter situations to find images fit to
describe his experience: he will see a stone, a slug, a puddle;
he will seize on that and with the metaphysical intuition of
the mystic will use it to marry the world of the familiar, the
everyday, with the unseen and visionary world of imagination,
re-creating that moment of perception.

In the following collection of poems, Juliet Gowan
successfully describes moments of intense inner understanding
and intuition in terms of the relentlessly day-to-day experiences
that press in on her. She explores and shares an inner life, both

suffering and joy-filled, through images of apparent triviality: 'Slug in the Wet', 'Bedsocks', 'Chestnut Trees' and 'Diggers' are really only the doors that open onto an inner life of searching, questioning, acceptance or rebellion; onto deeply loving relationships or encounters with pain or with a puzzling and confusing sense of personal inadequacy, or of delight in the quirkiness of the things visible.

Exploration of this personal inner world is not the only aim of the poems. 'The Old Ladies' is a tenderly drawn description of the difficulties of ageing. It is objective in its approach, but towards the end the poet moves into abstract considerations, and from the point of view of a still young woman she reflects on the universal challenge of coming to terms with old age; and on what seem vanishing qualities, known to an earlier generation. Mechanical diggers in a gravel pit epitomize workers' delight in exercising their special skill – though from time to time at the mercy of potentially disastrous fluctuations in the water table of life.

Some poems are grouped (see Notes) to explore individual themes: such are the 'Digger' poems or those of 'Chestnut Trees'. There are two sets of important, deeply felt poems, the 'Cathy' and 'Denis' poems, in both of which a personal experience of loving friendship cut short by death gives rise to anguished questioning about the meaning of pain and bereavement.

Moving and articulate in their personal grief, these two sets of poems also convey a sense of universal pain and loss. Reading the 'Cathy' poems when they first appeared in *The Critical Quarterly* in the 1960s so moved me that, although I had not yet met and made friends with Juliet Gowan, I felt urged to write on the same theme myself, in some way responding to this cry of pain, through some sense of empathy with it and all pain world-wide.

But the poems do not lead exclusively to deep and universal

questioning: in the tradition of the metaphysical poets, vivid images drawn from everyday life linger in the mind as a source of pleasure long after the 'meaning' of the poem has faded from memory. A slithery peach melba at Knutsford Service Station; an idle mechanical digger poised above its mirrored image on a watery gravel pit; the wild flowers surrounding Cathy's grave, or the sound of a cricket game, remembered from a childhood pram – these and countless other vivid moments serve to evoke in the reader's mind delight and wonder and a joyous awareness of the details of life around us. They open windows onto a landscape of mystery which – sometimes dimly, sometimes urgently – is thus revealed, beyond what we see and know.

Those of us who treasure our poetic inheritance of metaphysical and mystical poetry, who look on Herbert, Donne, Blake and many others as the foundations of our own powers of poetic imagination, will welcome this volume. It draws on much of the tradition and legacy of the past while using the language and idiom of our own times. We bless the poetic gift that can awaken our own awareness; so that we too, like Hardy, are enabled to 'notice such things'.

April O'Leary
Spring 2002

ACKNOWLEDGEMENTS

In these attempts to record as accurately as possible what one sees and what one glimpses lying behind or beyond – I am conscious of an incalculable debt to countless writers who appear to be dead, but clearly are not – so long as we have their wonderful work in our minds. I would like to list them but there are so many.

I am deeply grateful to all the following:

To my family and also to my husband, who has endured it all and helped in many ways, despite his conviction that life is history and not poetry! If he pronounces a new poem 'logical', I breathe again – 'logical' means more than one might think!

To friends who have read and responded faithfully over the years (including John Steane, expert in literature and music, sometimes scanning my poems over his cornflakes).

To John and Rosamond Peirson, whose years of loyal friendship included an earlier collection of my poems, put together to cheer me up when I was particularly ill.

To Tom Barnes who read the poems closely and made helpful suggestions on running order, to Ian Ramsey whose IT/technical assistance was invaluable, and to Richard Cook whose typography and jacket artwork design have been informed by a most sensitive understanding.

To Sister April O'Leary – a writer of memorable poetry – for agreeing to write the Foreword in 'that other harmony' of her prose.

Finally to Philip Rees, my godson (and later, stepson) and his fiancée, Anne Owen, who together planned and worked towards the publication of this book. Both have managed it and its author with wondrously equal parts of humour, efficiency and sensitivity.

For Geoffrey Chaucer

Propped on his elbow, where the cows had grazed,
With eyes that gleamed and twinkled, almost gloating,
Stout Chaucer lay and gazed and gazed,
And hardly mocked himself for doting.
O Professors, barn-owl-eyed and wordy,
In the heart of the greatest Clerk there grew a daisy,
Close to the ground, with a merry face, and sturdy.
All day it tracked the sun around the sky,
And when night came it quickly winked its eye.
And Chaucer knew it was not brave, and laughed,
    and told us why.

In Defence of Not putting my Poems into any Order other than Chronological

Meadow – here a harebell, there a thistle,
A leaf that has fallen early from its tree,
The mark of the worm upon it like a cross –
So rich a tangle, in which frog, cricket and bee,
Finding their ways through the grass with fumble and whistle,
Busy and awkward, calm the sense of loss
As I look at the backward rock.
Each thing, mysteriously complete, flung down
In warm confusion to grapple over this ground,
To stand, to stumble, to cherish and fight,
        To coil and unlock.

Beauty. The Beast. The complex light.
        The confronting and shock.

Loving and Wrecking: Spring Storm

Running athwart the wind
I was trying to head for harbour,
Knowing a light was beckoning there for me.
But the wind had other plans in mind
And grew momently fiercer and harder,
And the waves towered and beat me back out to sea.

Baffled but full of hope,
I tugged at the sheet, went about,
And was almost within that sheltering arm once more,
When suddenly, everything broke.
The light, it seems, has gone out.
And there are no messages from the shore.

Morning comes, grey and cold.
I should struggle, my bearings to find,
But the seas still pile and drive me wherever they will.
I mend the tackle and hold
My sail to the dregs of the wind.
I think not of harbour. My spirit lies battered and still.

Inland, the crocuses blow
In gardens out of the wind.
Wreckage lies littered – but will be cleared away.
I creep in, numbed and slow,
Accepting whatever relief I can find.
What can I bear from the storm into this day?
That I loved, and you drove me away.

Churchyard

I want to think about death and I do not want to think about it.
I want to think because it is now so important
To find you, Cathy. Cathy.

I rang the hospital to ask how you were
And could I come tomorrow, and take you out for the evening?
There was a pause.
      I suddenly felt cold.

And the voice I knew said gently
Oh my dear, I'm afraid we have bad news.
Heavy, blunt, the thing fell,
Quickened my ears and cut off my voice at the throat
Savagely, so I could hear but not speak.
I listened, and knives of pain
Ripped up the sudden cold silence inside me
Where morning and evening and close to me wherever I went
There had been voices pleading your need
And my love.
But now it was choking, it was impossible
To make any reply to the kindly, sorrowful voice with the knives.

Cathy's mother says, When I go out
I seem to be looking. In the evenings I want
To run outside and search up and down
In the streets to find her.

Where? That is what everyone always says.
Drowned. O where? cries Laertes,
(As if one could run to the place and snatch time back
And the dead with it)
And the Queen's answer is lengthy, and soothing
As plaster for a wound, but not as relevant.
      I do not care
Though a willow grows aslant the canal
Where you went, my Cathy.
If I had been there I would not have been seeing the willow.
When I was with you I never used to have much
Time for anything else but you.
Your grim jokes, your funny smile, your courage
And the endless futility of your pain
That curbed and dragged one's heart.
No, I should not have been seeing the willow
Though afterwards I might perhaps have remembered it
Being an emblem
Of grief. What matters is where you are now.

So I went to Wales, to the little church
Overlooking the sea.
I had brought primroses, but the primroses grew wild there.
The evening spread out gravely over the sea.
I could tell at once where I had to go,
For the white flowers were luminous
And there were so many white flowers.
So I knelt and balanced the primroses carefully
Not being able to see very well –
      And the wild ones were lovelier anyway –
But this was not how I meant to come, Cathy –
Not bringing flowers to your grave.

In words, so gently, we wrap the dead up. It is an act
Of beatification, as natural to us
As breathing is, or burial. It empearls
Our hurt and our hope. It is a last gesture
From a new loneliness. We turn
And there are no more gestures to make. You are gone.
As surely as balm or embalmment
The words heal, they are covering and calm.

I must rip it up.
Words, you distance her, lulling me. I am afraid.
I do not want to lose her under all the sweet flowers.
So you, fine words, keep away till I have done thinking.
I want to think, about Death.
I want to think because it is now so important
To keep you. Cathy. Cathy.

Cathy: Oxford

If I had been there I should not have been seeing the willow,
Nor even the deep clover in the meadow
Or tiny speedwell down by the place where you went –
Now there is only these flowers to watch.
I watch them float, watch the dark water beneath them –
Ache at your cry from the dark.

Lift your eyes and the meadow is bright with sun.
The trees stand round gravely, their sympathy quiet and attentive.
This is the place I shall come back to;
Or it will come back to me –
Beginning with royal clover deep in the meadow,
And this flower of speedwell touching the cheek of the stream.

'How Should I Your True-love Know?'

Everything on the stage is charcoal gray,
Filigreed with long silver tears of rain.
    From where I sit in the dark pit's angle
        Below the actors,
    They are larger, much larger than life –
They loom, and the grave is enormous,
Like the monstrous figure of Hamlet's father.

Then the Queen with golden hair stoops over the open grave,
    Just as I am thinking, Cathy, Cathy –
And Hamlet, too, suddenly realises who it is in there,
And cries out, hiding his head in Horatio's shoulder.
And I am shocked and shaken into crying,
For there they lower Ophelia, all Ophelias, all my Cathys,
    Everyone's in the world, we cry, we cry –
Because of the primroses dropped from the great Queen's hand
    Like meteors into Pluto's desperate kingdom.

Landscape with Snow

In this land, this time and season,
When the snow has fallen and not melted,
And the light is not convinced where the land is,
Or which is the sky
Or the fields, or the empty air,
Each tree is now a stranger to its neighbour,
And stands so – taut, withdrawn, like you –
Until I come there;
And its loneliness looks up and holds me –
Challenges my stare.

When I drive along these roads that I know,
That we went on together,
I am aware of you, of course,
But, islanded in lights and noise,
I can be reached by other roads and weather;
I can be traced by roads I have not known,
By trees standing alone.
Then I leave these ones and go
Into the wilderness your home –
Into your land of grey light and snow,
Like despair –
I recognise the landmarks and I come
And meet you there.

'This City Now…'

Autumn hunts you down, year after year,
Nudging you first with a red flag in a morning lane
Hung out, stiff, in the mist –
Little sounds: the crunch of an apple –
Faint smells: bonfire smoke. Chrysanthemums. Dusk.
It's been padding after you ever since your first,
Your very first party, in the first dark evening
In your best frock, white socks, clean hanky,
Present for hostess heavy in your hand – excitement.
   Already, already
   Nostalgia.
Edwardian, Victorian feelings – even then.
      Already
Looking back. An ache. A luxury of dying. Very strange.

It'll get you, somewhere. Will it be here, under the plane trees
In the Mall? Under those clustered bobbles
   Hung… in the mist, in the air.
So quiet. Or in Trafalgar Square?
Where a red bus looms and is gone again,
Traffic is coming and fading; a taxi one side moves
Unknown to a taxi the other side. Blinkers on everyone.
Mystery. Who is in there? *Who is there?*
Someone is waiting, just breathing, born.
Prince Charming – is he at the party?

People are back at work now, after the scattered summer,
Things of importance can happen here: meetings, planning,
Ideas. Idea of a party, idea of a city.
Brisk, morning mist. A tough, resilient season,
Deliberately concealing its plans for spring.
People have got to be deceived by the bobbles,
The dustcarts, the oceans of leaves, the echoes and yearning
The nudgings, the isolation, the mist, the ache,
The backward tugging and drawing to Christmas, December.
(These months that keep ending in 'ember' –
Such echoes. Such whispers. Such hiding in corners.
                                        Remember.)
The hunting goes on, dogging your muffled footsteps.
Someone, something for you, in the mist. Exciting.

It may be here, in Malet Street, by this new building
… Empty as yet, but pleasing, with pillars and overhang,
Waiting for autumn term, young people, couples
Meeting for the first time, immemorially, round these corners,
These pillars, with vistas through – unusual in London –
To yellowing leaves, old, terraced houses,
Plane trees, and Novembers in all great cities.
(This world, this world, has it always been old?
– Since its very first party, at three, or four?
A big, brass knocker on the door.
Welcome, and lights, and delight –
Your present, so very important, so mysterious,
So full of hope. You look up from the wrapping, a little child
A la recherche du temps perdu…)

It is best to be a new building in autumn.
You quickly become old, with piles of leaves
In all your rawest, newest angles.
These leaves have always known they would one day be old.
They meet it with such singular resignation. They seem to love it.
They accept drifts, and even dustcarts.
And the plane trees in Russell Square, they are big, and old, and beautiful.
'An unusual collocation of words' says a sensitive African,
Willing, but not quite able, to understand.
For the trees in his childhood, though big, and old,
And no doubt beautiful also in their way,
Could not know an English November. November in such a city.
Nor an English child's shiver and thrill,
Waiting for the door to open on the party –
Rustling of paper, and autumn leaves – and already
      A chill.
Already a sense of heaviness – of wanting to lie
Beneath a cover of leaves on the cold ground,
And be unwrapped, discovered at last, accepted – found.

Psst! Here's the Key. The Gang's Waiting!
(Malet Street in June)

Under lamp standards in London, and snug at the feet of the meters,
Weeds have parked without paying, and are delightedly welcomed.
    Yellow and raffish, saucy and cockney and gay.
Wet-the-bed, chickweed, shepherd's purse, delicate milkmaid –
Truant hands start down in greeting – then pull guilty away,
Looking round for the everywhere warden, who guards all this formal and
    grey.
         He isn't here today.
         Perhaps you can stay –
         Perhaps we can play!

'...Destiny, that hath to instrument this lower world...'

We are waiting at quiet nine-thirty Whitechapel.
The Tube doors are open, and
The patient people on train and platform
Mutually self-conscious.

The guard looks at his watch.
Time yet.

Down the stairs trips an elegant little black man.
His clothes are pressed, well-cut, his umbrella impeccably rolled.
He is, perhaps, a king in his own country.
He thinks he has just caught the train.
What luck! He steps neatly aboard.
But is it going to the destined place?
There are two lines. Where is the indicator?
Perhaps the train – he stands irresolute in the doorway –
Has other places in mind, may even
Hurry him violently off in an opposite direction!

Calm yourself. It IS New Cross you want, little man.
And this IS the train.
He recovers his poise.
Looks imperiously at his watch, and then at the guard.
Why does the train not move? I am quite ready!
Home, James! Do you not know a king when you see one?
(Or at least a future Cabinet Minister).

The guard unhurriedly moves inside
And the train glides away.
On the back we can see the legend
'Earl's Court'. Upside down. Like a wink.

New Estate

Along a broad, grey street, the lamplight falls.
Twilight on suburbia. Low brick walls,
And shrubs in gardens that are newly dug.
No sound. Only a stillness that seems suspended
As if an old, deep passion just has ended,
Or under anaesthetic a pain lies drugged.
What is this pain that lurks in the godless lamplight?
– This ache and ecstasy, brimming the quiet heart?
Is it desire, to know the end of the waiting
– The bringing to birth, or the tired fall back to the start?
No sound; no answer. The twilight lies without motion.
A small mist shrouds the secret ecstasy there.
And always the twilight, mist and shadow are weaving
A magic, a mystery – why do I fear to share?

Covenant

Why are chestnuts, for me, such arks of promise, apart?
    Is it because, more than all other trees,
They are nearly dark at their heart,
    And hold up candles, briefly, to catch the heat?

Yes, for a moment in May, as soon as they know
    This warm gloom to be so,
They cover themselves with candles that stand and glow
    Against their leaves.

    And then absorb these gleamers, and grow
    More and more leafy, more and more deep,
    Stiller. More authoritative. Like Sleep.

God's Language

At last we have come to the year's deep centre,
      And under chestnut gloom I move, to find –
If words will come and lodge within my mind –
What secret here lies hidden where so few will enter.
      (Ideas are often shadowy. Perhaps there are no words.)

Outside, in the fields and heat, amid nettle and dandelion,
      My mind would have to move about, accepting, rejecting;
In here, canopied from the sky, I can accept everything,
And am, completely, accepted. This is my pavilion.
      (Ideas can settle. Yet there is no one word.)

Judgment was such a burden. In here, I want to dance
      Slowly, in thought, balancing, blindly recognizing.
These leaves, like hands, press my eyes into silence
And hold me to other, more delicate modes of perceiving.
      (Ideas are alive, and moving. But, still, no words.)

Spread your hands out, feel the playing light,
      The searching warmth and wind, finding leaf after leaf.
I know what is above me, this relief
Of gloom and shadows, mercifully bordering my restless sight.
      (Ideas are winged. They house here independently of words.)

The trunk of this tree is so huge I cannot get my arms around it.
      Its leaves were the first ones out to assure me stickily of spring.
One knew no frosts could stop those sturdy buds from opening,
Those spreading hands from placing shade where I have found it.
      This is not now an idea. It is a tent, a court, a home –
      A loving prison. And these are the words.

'Oure Hooste'

Chestnut is a jovial, social tree –
His leaves are clustered in such warm, convivial groupings.
Host-hearted, he invites the company,
Provides the jocund feast, and we come trooping.
Each leaf, in heavy pleasure, like a bee,
Hangs from the honey-tower with lobe-like drooping.
In here then, here's the doorway, follow me.
Don't mind the dark: don't mind the need for stooping
To reach the rich distilment of the inn –
To stand upright and welcome as a guest within.

Seeing and Catching

Chestnuts over a pond. Dank and still.
Shafts of morning sun dive under and through
Piercing the leaves translucently from below.
    Emerald, dazzling...

Chestnut trees in the evening. The lengthening light
Picking out this little party of leaves, and that –
Intensifying their clusters against the dark...

Chestnuts in November. A bonfire of gold
More royal than Kings' Fireworks on Gunpowder Night
Streaming up – to burst in the purple sky...

Chestnut buds in August in pairs at the tip of a twig,
Ready for next spring, like pointed breasts
Between arms and fingers spread wide and bold and handsome,
    like a child's drawing of Mum,
      all eyes – in the wrong place? – and hands.

Convalescent

Look how calmly the sunlight lies on that white wall,
Late in the afternoon, listening to the birds.
Does it hear as I hear – that warm, unwinking sunlight?
Can it, too, hear in the birdsong sweet familiar words?

Hush, don't disturb that sunlight with your thinking.
Even as I write, it fades and shadows fall.
Just, with no thought, lie and watch it gleaming
At the birds' teatime song on the whitewashed wall.

Trouble in Mind

You walked those sunlit stones and hills
   So long ago.
I walk so complex and so lonely now.
Can feet so certain trace these paths of doubt?
Can hands nailed down to fact grope in this wood despair
   And draw me out?
I reach for you across two thousand years of air,
And, turning, find that you were here, and now.
   A bird drops into air:
   Life breathes and fills.

Dies Irae: Slug in the Wet

Here's a peaceful sight: a slug on a slate.
Bemused by so much rain, awash in a little pool,
   Lengthened and mild he lies –
   Laid out, relaxed, like a cat,
    But pearly and cool,
     And his eyes
    Move this way and that
   In leisurely, drunk surprise.

The sun will come out. The tiny slug will wait.
He doesn't even remember the doomsday late
   night's lashing and hate.
    He is cleared, immaculate.

Spring-Fall

I danced by the first daffodil in the wind.
I was stirred in the earth of my mind.
I swung on a tree. Hyperbole.
And you said, Be calm. You were kind.
    I was blind.
Despair came dragging behind.

Poets

Fish, in the dark, moving water,
You balance and confront the water with patience.
Perhaps if I could swim with you,
    Belly to belly,
Sharing your skill, your effortless primeval patience,
    I could be cured.

Involvement

Unquiet heart, you'll never know
What that stock-dove does for you –
What he has that makes him coo
    So deep, and hurt, and true.

Sunlight lies on evening leaves;
Traffic noises dwindle, slow.
Lazy all my thoughts, and now
    The stock-dove murmurs, low.

Evening sky a deepening blue,
Bordered by the darkened eaves;
Sunlit, somewhere, stock-dove grieves,
    And what he loves, believes.

Thoughtful in the after-glow,
Capture him and keep him so –
Throaty, velvet, tranquil grow
    Like him – then you'll know.

Plastic Surgery

And who is going to iron out the faces
Of these terrible, neurotic London buses?
And even if one could, what good would it do?
They'd just be smooth, expressionless and out of pain.

No trace of the older friendliness and dignity remaining
These new ones are frightening, and would be more so,
Battered, not by experience, but by tranquillisers –
The damage deadlier because below the surface –
More savagely defeated. Bland. Inane.

'Nous n'irons plus aux bois: les lauriers sont coupés'

I cannot place this empty sky
This raping light that leaves the lilies staring
It seems that every bud was born to freeze.
Exposure. They have cut down all my trees.

The lake is full and still; the streams weep ice.
Only the honeysuckle now is baring
A green so cool, so self-possessed and blue,
It can't foretell that rampant golden hue
That it should soon be wearing.
After this Lent, God knows what June can do.
The birds ravage the buds so silently.

I am afraid to look, afraid to find
This void must take its place within my mind
And disinherit seasons warm and blind.

Hot

Oh God I am hot, heavy and hot, too hot.
I wish I were cool, cool at my root, like a vine,
Still, and bearing a grape – translucent, luscious –
      For wine.
      But I'm not.
I'm walking about, and I have no root,
      And I'm hot.

Ache

I thought you were gone for good and I did not care.
    Then I remembered, suddenly, unexpectedly,
Reading an isolated poem, how you had talked
So warmly about Emily Dickinson. Listening, I was aware
Of the huge rough hole you had left, and that it hasn't healed.

My eyes went up from the page to the grey window
And the noise of drills in the street, enquiring their meaning;
And I couldn't help noticing – I didn't mean to,
But I couldn't help noticing, that in this room
    There are too many empty chairs,
And only one person – a stranger – about whom
    I do not know, or care.

However I shovel to fill up the hole with words,
    The edges are jagged and bare,
And the drilling pain, the shudder is still there.

Pilgrimage of Princes

Christ of the Cross and the Easter garden,
Prince of the early morning light and the first primrose
Lord of that tearful laughter and rest
   from which we came
And towards which we are going,
You have our inward gratitude, gravity,
Marvel, allegiance, devotion.

But only this Babe at his glowing hearth
Amid tingling frosty carols in the clear air,
Only this little Lord Jesus in his manger –
Pilot Lord of the snowflake, wick of the candle flame,
Bright woody berry deep in the pagan holly,
Apple deliciously groped-for in the stocking,
Bell in the trembling steeple, Birth in the winter night –
Can melt us to loving and wonder, can kindle, enclose us
In warmth and delight.

Each Year

When it comes round to Christmas again we shall sing carols –
Lovely, rocking carols, like falling snow.
Thank God for the fall of the year, for the fall of the snow
Eddying down the lamplight at a quiet station,
Hushing us towards Christ's crisp, white mass and his warm manger.

Reliquary

This heavy casket of gold, inwrought with diamond and pearl,
    And lined with delicate silk, encloses
        A treasure –
    The light, exhausted bone of a saint –
        My treasure,
    Lapped around with delicate silk, enclosed
By heavy gold, inwrought with radiant pearl.

Thunder

God speaks in thunder.
Lucky God.
I wish I could.

Snow in March

This is a corner of winter that no one will look at and wonder.
They just say 'Oh, it's the snow. Let it go. Take it away.
Let it be May, no more snow. Let us play: Go away go.'
This, to the sudden six inches of snow, that can still
Kindle the eyes of the elderly ticket collector
At his station so tiny and new
Standing firm, square and true
With the trains drifting dreamily through
And the snow drifting too.

Time is a dream of the tall University clock –
For the settling snow and the snow-blocked branches between
Will not let it be seen.
And the thoughts of the folk on the seat in the waiting-room shift,
Float and settle, like voyaging birds on a boat far adrift,
As the dark sea around
Swallows thought, swallows sound.

So here all the six of us sit - in the innocent light
In this magical corner of winter – breathless and white
Not a word
Is uttered or heard
Till the train comes in sight
And we silently file to our cushiony seats in the train,
Each one lost, each one living again.

Selfhood (Cloning)

Disturbed by duplicate frogs in an Oxford laboratory,
I take time off from reading the Sunday papers
To wonder how I should feel, what strange excitement,
If, after all this incredible loneliness,
The world should suddenly contain a group
Of duplicate me's.

All this effort to understand myself,
To adapt my kind of living to the rest –
To change what's hard or weak, develop and test
Ideas against experience. To cling
So centrally to what I value, once I know what it is –
And all that process of finding it – all this
To be shared. A group's experience. Nothing finally lost
By a failure in one direction. Always the others to turn to,
To see what one meant all the time. No misunderstanding –
Oh God, no misunderstanding! Not to have to explain!

All this limitation from living in one country,
Loving one set of wildflowers from my childhood,
Knowing only one framework of customs and laws –
Always wondering, what if I had been born
Into *that* household? All this silent debate
Now to be so boldly external, so articulate.

Marriage. Oh my goodness, what a problem.
Do we find a perfect matching group
Of males of equal number? What if one is missing,
And one of us has to be the Old Maid? No babies. Always an aunt.
Solve that one if you can. I can't.

Within the group, would there be polarization
Of angel and black sheep – Conscience? Humility? Pride?
Would social instincts, capacity for loving
Be shared among us. Or be all on one side?

We could admire each other, approve of our better actions –
Actually, I do rather like freckles –
You're looking jolly today.
Pity each other – that was a tough assignment.
Various happenings in my life have hurt me.
Knowing everything, though, would forgiveness be possible?
Or would the burden of shame be just as heavy?

Have there always been, in my mind, these other tadpoles
Squirming along beside me? What is it we have shared?
What is this deep thing we are all so sure of,
That I have never been able to explain to anyone –
This rooted, shade-under-a-summer-tree identity?
This sliding, watercress-on-gravel love.
They/we must all be sure of it. Am I glad?
The idea does strike me like gladness. But would I be
Really happy never to be alone? – If I am alone now, with this
        infernal conscience! –
And what about God and me?
Does he love each one of the group so specially?
Obviously he does. No change there: we're all prized equally –
But forgiven? died for? found? – individually?

Would ideas strike us separately,
And be passed round the group for rejection or comment?
Or would they come to us all at once –
So we'd meet on Sunday and say without preliminaries,
Well, what do you think?
Or would we simply proceed to action, without thought
Or communication; no, that would be dull.
I like reflection. So presumably, do the others;
And it seems as if that would be, ultimately –
And may have been from the start –
 What all this is about.
A groping, growing. A potter throwing –
 Debating with his art.
An image glowing. Language for knowing.
 A writing and acting one's part.
An echo and a listening round a shout.
 A working out.

The Gentle Rain: A Villanelle

The rain falls softly through the tree.
She nothing harsh contains nor keen,
But bears a gentle memory.

Washed down the years of history,
Cleansed by many a changing scene
The rain falls softly through the tree.

And though she come from some far sea
Unpure, yet holds she nothing mean,
But bears a gentle memory.

And, faced with strife, she bends her knee.
Since she in many a storm has been,
The rain falls softly through the tree.

Sighing softly, falling free,
Gently turning grey to green –
The rain falls softly through the tree;
She bears a gentle memory.

Illumination

Oyster, bedded in ooze, grating on heart of pearl,
  Fashioning purity out of irritation,
Listen to me where you lie on the sea's bed, for I love you.
  And want to have a conversation about love.

'Pearl is the prison-warder of my pain.'
'Pain is the jealous guardian of my pearl.'
'Pain is the stronger and will out and away.'
'Pearl is the stronger and will contain
      For ever and ay.'
'And Beauty?' – 'Beauty may blossom from both, may unfurl,
  Still to grow, still to stay.'

The Violin Tries to Understand False Relation

There's something here I keep on teasing at, helplessly but persistently,
Too complex a structure for my one-track wit
That thinks in tunes, not harmony or fugue.
Does it matter that I can't understand it?
(*The pear tree is in bloom outside my window*)
It must, or I wouldn't keep returning.

That you were kind to me, and now you misinterpret me and hurt me –
That's the first level of mystery I can't fathom.
That I still love you, and am bound to you more strongly by your strong
    unkindness –
That's the second. That I want to comfort *YOU*.

That God must suffer this, every second of every minute of every day
Since Calvary. How can he bear it? I think I should go mad.
And yet he doesn't. And I don't either.

That terrible locked door.
               – (*outside, outside my window*)
I did think the key was Love. But either the word
Means something else that I don't know yet,
Or eternity is not open either, but there are mansions in it
Where a person can go in, and shut himself in,
And hurl the key at the stars.
And we shall sit outside here, waiting, perhaps for ever.

I suppose we shall talk – about you. You won't like that, will you?
So much pain might evaporate under our scrutiny,
And you'd be left with so little to steer by –
One star, certainly, in the North.

But somehow I don't think we shall. Love has more tact than that
And a longing to preserve the individual delicacy.
That, at all costs, is what must be cherished.

*I would go away forever if it would prove to you that I love you
and do not want to hurt you.*

But my instinct is to go on affirming this music –
(Which would not sound the same if we were apart) –
Soundlessly, listening...
And to stay as close to you
As the bars will permit.
The pear tree fruit sets painfully inside my heart.

Two Library Ghosts

Yesterday, although we've said goodbye
And that's all finished, you were in the library.
Only there for an hour myself, I watched you
Out of the corner of an eye, loving and wary
And working, and not stirring from my desk.
Today you are not here, and I know why.

These months that lie ahead, how can I bear
To look across this busy room to where
Your grey head bending studious to a book
Would lift for me with that warm friendly look
I knew too briefly, shall not know again.

There's only one solution to this pain:
That I should go across and take your place
In that corner where we used to talk so often –
You tipping back your chair to turn and greet me –
Me bringing thoughts and finds I had to share.

Yes, I could go and study in that chair.
Then, from that known but unfamiliar angle,
The new ghost in this room where we were happy
Would be my other self that holds your hand.
Will your ghost understand?

Bedsocks

I can't ever get to sleep if my feet are cold,
So I take my bedsocks with me wherever I go.
    I met a lady who didn't want to love God.
    She said so. We agreed about the need
    For warm feet if one is to get one's rest.
    She said 'I haven't brought my bottle, and anyway
    The water here is cold.'
    I said 'What you need is some bedsocks –
    Then you wouldn't need to worry about the bottle
    Or the water.' I would have lent her mine
    But she clearly wouldn't have thought it was hygienic.
    I was very sorry for her,
    Lying awake in the dark with her numbed feet
    And her soul.
But obviously I wasn't sorry enough,
Or I would have been able to do something for her –
Not just be smug about my own bedsocks.

Oh lady, the cold of your feet does hurt God so.

Incommunicado

Sounds of a cricket game. A sunny day.

The warm sides of my pram, the dangling fringe
Of the canopy over my head. The person pushing.
Toys that are mine to fondle or throw away,
And are always – mysteriously – returned. The pillow's hushing.
The steady, leisurely rolling of wheels below me.
     Trees, people passing.
A world that can be ignored, need not impinge,
Nor even know me –
So confident am I it is all my own.

     The pram is now outgrown.
Walking beside it I am amazed
     At the imperious, glazed
Look on that rosy, canopy-dappled face.
I bend to speak to you and am met with a frown.
Stammering, I retire. I know my place –
     A world away.

The Old Ladies

Old lady, creaking upstairs to your room in the final club,
Do you know what a stumbling block you are to me, in my thought?
Not just because I want so much to get past you
And am schooling myself to patience behind your back.
India and your husband climb beside you,
And they stand, as you do, dimly but firmly
      For something I lack.

A strange new whirling way of life has flung you –
Obsolete, resentful, marvellously polite –
To face such problems as transference of weight
From stair to stair, from joint to swollen joint,
Or how to cook one tomato and one rasher
On a gas ring soon too low for you to stoop to...

Connie dear, you used to be my problem,
Dwindling in your bed like a puff of down –
So heavy-light, it needed a system of pulleys
To get you up above the bed to be changed.
So knotted, so sunk in upon yourself
     – Old-Man-of-the-Sea Arthritis twenty years
     Your brutal bedfellow –
You seemed one with those intricate string bags
You tangled with such soft determination,
Until those feather-light claws dropped suddenly quiet,
      And I missed you, your warm room,

Your insistence on a real coal fire,
Your spindly, dignified letters,
Beautiful calm manners,
Rigorous light-blue eyes –
Courage, tranquillity, courage.

Unchained to plot we shall perish.
The story will have no true and proper end
Until we are defined at length by death.
When all the obscure logic of our lives,
The intricate reference systems, painful punctuation,
Discipline of grammar, memory, thought,
Attraction of like and opposite, indecision,
Panic, confusion, then decision again –
When all this is done, and has been rightly recorded,
We too can turn to the stairs and creak to bed,
With something of this obstinate, tortoise courage
In the shape of an old lady, going ahead.

'Briar Rose'

An eight-year-old child is suspended 'in ice',
in the hope of an ultimate cure for her cancer.
New Year 1972.

A little child sleeps in a crystal –
Watch us, child.
Secret of canker, patience, hope –
Keep your watch over us.
You, the guardian of our painful years,
From your terrible crystal will give us judgment.

The alien needle pricked.
A drop of blood. There
She lies, asleep in the castle.
Asleep her court around her,
Asleep her father and mother,
Asleep her maids.
The cooks in the kitchen; all sleep.
How beautiful. How still.
Cobwebs float, useless.
No fly stirs.

Only imagination
               moves
Here, like an eye, in the silence
Watching the hedge grow –
Bramble, briar, wild rose.
Imagination knows
The validity of silence
The validity of the rose.
Knows that the time will pass,
The spell be broken at last.
A hundred years.
               A hundred years.

Must we wait that long for the cure?
We shall all be dead and forgotten.
The canker you fell asleep with –
Hate, like a briar hedge, round you –
Ireland, the bombs, the clamour –
Will all be over, forgotten,
A backward cloud in the crystal.
A clot of blood on the needle.

If the world could be stilled by ice–?
    It has happened before.
If the angry world could be stilled
    And await the cure.

A hundred years.
    In the story,
The cook went on clouting the scullion.
Was the Prince's journey for this?
And his vision, and his kiss?

And they also tell us the story
Of the girl with the silver saucer
And the twirling, transparent apple,
In which she could see the world.
She was murdered in the forest
For the sake of her silver saucer
For the sake of her transparent apple.
But there grew a reed from her grave,
And it sang and told her story,
And they dug her up and brought her
To life with the holy water.

And do you also remember
Snow White, asleep in the forest?
Between her milk-white teeth
A bite of the poisoned apple.
The old witch laughed in the dark
But the dwarfs were there, were watching.

Now, little child in the ice,
Whoever made these tales
Made them for your sake.
If imagination fails,
    Do not wake.

Battering Rams

It is cold and clear on the battlements,
    And you talk of Strindberg and wars.
Your mind is ranging and free of the sky;
    But my spirit droops indoors.
I listen and wish I could reach you,
    But my spirit smiles and falls –
For my eyes are drawn by the snowdrops
    At the foot of the castle walls.

Cannon stand quiet around us.
    You talk of 'sex war' and Genet.
I do not think there's a war on,
    But I want to run down and play.
I want to run down the Hundred Steps
    And stand where the clear bugles call,
And the snowdrops are pushing up the brown leaves
    Under the castle wall.

Dominant

This tune is drifting, floating, coming home.
    You are silent now. I am alone.
Nothing I say can reach you where you are.
Not even so searching a love can pierce so far.
    I must be still and patient as a star.

Light years away from now and this love you may turn and see
How fiercely the image of you and your grief has been haunting me.
    And then you will stand and will come
    And after the years alone
    This will be home.
And there will never be an end to loving, never an end to knowing
    You as the dark, resonant heart of my star.

Currency

Identify a poem as something precious, unstable
  And interesting, which you want always to be
Where you can reach it. Under your hand. To have and to hold.
  Then how unhappy am I: my only poem is you,
  And you are so suddenly cold.
And all I can see is your loved, obstinate back,
  Stiff with resentment and pain –
    You, walking away.
  Yet loving you is a lack
With a strength and a value I cannot explain –
  Spendthrift, resilient, gay.

No one has ever been so precious to me –
  No one so interesting.
To say there never will be again
Sounds so extravagant. Markets are mysteries. How can one know?
  I hope there never will be another:
  I am jealous for your position
As my most cherished, costly possession –
Though you will never honour that word and must be
Current, unstable, even in memory.
Convert to me, prized and prodigal gold, some day.

Birds on a Quiet Evening

Their voices are free of the air as their light, winged bodies are:
    The echoes are at home there.
Twigs take them and bend as they ride to them and grip and sway:
    One touch and they are known there.
Tree trunks shoulder them and nests hollow cradling around them, for they
    So fittingly have flown there.
And watching them I too have longed to sing and fly and cling and sleep
    and pray –
    And never be alone, there.

Still Life – Pheasant

From under the dark yew tree, suddenly
   Out of the quiet and cold,
Spurring away
         over the leaves
          lacy with frost
   Crackles a pheasant
        ablaze
         aflame
  In scarlet-and-gold.

I see him run up a bank: he is part of the sunlight –
A rainbow realised in oils; he is part of the landscape.
   Momentary, heraldic, historical, exact,
   Alien, naturalized, a fact.
   Passant, on argent, emblazoned, on a field,
   Saracen Crusader, with a shield.
Accoutred for the tourney, lanced and low,
Across the frozen woods I hear his colours go.

   Crécy. Agincourt. An echo,
        An echo.

Aplomb

Bird, you are much too big for that sapling tree –
But I like to see you sitting there just the same.
      Your adult weight advances it dignity.

It thought it might grow up a bush, before you came –
      Or part of a hedge –
And was groping about for a gage of maturity.
Out of uncertain air you settled and gave it a name.
And the confident clasp of your claw is relief, and a pledge
      Of futurity.

An April Affair

Who would have thought that hail would come with these petals?
Will a hailstone ride like this through the air,
Mounting the petal like a velvet carpet?

When they land, he will bump and bruise her, gash her,
And then he will melt, and vanish away into air.

But the blue-veined bruise stays with her
To witness they rode together –
Engraved, his absent impact of presence there.

Recognition

I

Parting the buttercups that gild this meadow
I find the daisy I am looking for.
Laughing and shy, we know we found each other.

I hardly dare look up to see
If you are looking down at it, like me.

II

Seth, when the meadow is glutted with buttercups,
I run into it looking for one flower only.
It is the daisy that grows so close, so hidden in your heart,
    You do not seem to know that it is there.
But I must kneel to find this little darling –
Do not be afraid: I do not ask to keep it –
    We shall just look at each other.
There are no words for such sympathy.
Then I shall stand up again and go. I have places where I can go.

The daisy may notice that vanished, cherishing gaze.
Please do not let it grow lonely for ever.

Two Songs: One

I ask a question: you are silent.
Water is still; buds break, and wait.
It seems that in this landscape after all
The spring may not be going to happen.

You eat the bud I offer, trustingly.

Beyond, beyond, there lies the song of birds.

Song

for Aucassin and Nicolette

The sky is overcast and has no meaning –
    As we no words.
Down here beneath the beech tree, not up there,
Blue breaks in flowers, and the single pair
Of daffodils that stand and look like one
    Are Shakespeare and the sun.

At the breaking point of this defeating day
We have come through to music: I can say
I'll meet you in the garden at New Place
And take your hand and turn my head away
And still be where I love you face to face.

This garden be the guardian of the words –
This daybreak bordered by the songs of birds.

Doggerel

The Poodle and I keep settling down to snore –
But a poem comes: I keep having to turn the light on.

Several times he has almost opened the door –
This magazine cover is all I can find to write on.

The silly old ass keeps pushing it shut with his paw –
I think of a better word, and I turn the light on.

We do not think we can stand it any more.
O Muse, do you think you could possibly pass the 'light' on?

But the Poodle and I obey the Higher Law –
The dog leaps down again with a groan, and I turn the light on.

Pacific Ocean: A Villanelle

When it is over, I shall meet your eyes,
Widened, and bedded in new peacefulness –
Your lips, so soft with thanks, and glad surprise.

This face, so loved, could never tell me lies,
Never estrange me from your sharp distress.
When it is over, I must meet your eyes,

Your forehead, eyebrow: calm, these troubled skies.
My gentle finger moves to touch and bless
Your lips, so soft with thanks and glad surprise;

My loving hand, your hair. I realise
Anew the piercing peace of tenderness.
When it is over, I must meet your eyes.

Your questing hand lastly at anchor lies
On my sea-bed, rocking to steadfastness.
Your lips are soft with thanks, and glad surprise.

This precious cargo we have won, this prize
Is home, is harbour, brimmed with tranquilness.
When it is over, I must meet your eyes,
Your lips, so soft with thanks, and glad surprise.

On the Other Side

Here is 'Lavender Bower' in 'Mayflower Way' –
    Names thus richly begot
Upon a tight little lady by a crinoline card,
    And by a sad Town Clerk upon an autumn day.
Here are pink may and cherry which will bear no fruit
And the shimmering laburnums dropping death to children.

In the gutter flaps a photo of a real refugee
    With her baby bleeding in her arms – Don't shoot.
Christian Aid Week, 1966: we forgot.
The reporter, whoever he was, did not.

In the Land of the Parliaments

I remember a telegram from Hungary.
It said, why don't you come?
For God's sake help us, help us.
We didn't. The tanks rolled in,
And there were no more telegrams:
Nothing more was said.

I remember a cardinal they took
And shone lights at him until he broke
And said – of himself – what was not true.
Then he went into hiding in a dangerous place
Where God is iron Jailer –
The only way through.

Both these things I remember
So that Hungary now is a voice
Of silence and iron and caught movement;
Theirs to us, cut off under crawling iron;
Ours to them – a movement of the heart
Choked by centuries of being fair
To charters, of considering
All consequences. Not acting swiftly
By the heart. When moved, not speaking.

Travelling North

Frightened by Yorkshire, deadened by County Durham,
After so many bleak fields and stiff, silly sheep,
Dr Johnson and I are thankful to reach the suburbs,
Savour the little back gardens, some being dug,
Some displaying with pride the results of digging –
Or the battered trike left out, or the dolls' tea party
Strewn on the grass in favour of beans and jam
At five o'clock – or the sudden surprised-looking fireplace
Propped up against the back shed, waiting for Steptoe.
Signs of life, and the world is more than sheep.

Now, Newcastle in evening sunlight, grand.
Heavy over the bridge, and tall red chimneys.
Dirt and the soot are workmen here,
Part of the civic disdain:
(Southerner, shove on North in your clean blue train.)

Grand, and the train noses and clanks and shudders
Finding the lines out for going North.
Suddenly gaining assurance
We master the line and are free.
Northumberland comes – like a wind-picked pearl –
        Holy Island. The sea.

Longing

I want to go on a great calm lake,
    But the lake has a shore.
I want to go on the open sea –
    But even then I want more.
For the seas of the world are round, are round
And the sea that I want, in my mind, in my mind,
    Has no bound, has no bound.
And my soul's boat goes, it journeys on
    Into sight, into sound.

Late Christening

Like a newly-surfaced road,
My life is empty now,
And clean, smooth.

Exciting –
Dangerous, perhaps?
There are no white lines.

The emptiness makes me afraid,
Nags me greyly,
Like toothache
Or responsibility.

Knutsford Service Centre

Staring through vast glassiness of the restaurant,
Still almost riding, almost part of the motorway –
Buzzing in the head, a dim, floating feeling –
One is only convalescent, not yet cured.

Cheshire with its odd, squashed trees sits round in the rain,
In the slow grey waves asserting its own identity,
Its sense of being a settlement, belonging.
Fenced in, isolated here, condemned to motion,
We may not share this poise.

Grappling with peach melba's sun and snow,
Trying to get a purchase on its slither,
I feel my seat swivelling me away –
Here, you are only welcome if you are going.

I move towards the exit – polewards only –
Grateful for stabilizing steak, and coffee.
Thank you, Knutsford, for a kingly gesture
    And a poem.

Crazy Bird

Crazy bird, you perched on my tree
you even made a home here
nested for six years
home-on-the-dot.
Then you pole-vaulted off
on your fifth leg
into the sky
and I don't know, I don't know
where you are
trilling and harping
now.
Abraham's bosom?

I might go crazy myself you know
here in this tree
without you?
Where for instance, is *my* fifth leg?
In the ashtray
comes a piping voice.
Ah, that is true.

No. Don't let words
blow your mind.

You weren't really crazy.
You were the sanest little bird
I ever met.
Oh let me not be mad, not mad, sweet heaven!
Keep me in temper, I would not be mad.

'Remember me! But ah, forget my fate!'

Thus Dido, and she stabs herself and dies.
I sang Dido once.
They said it was impossible
to make 'this face' (mine)
look like a tragedy queen.
So I gave up and looked
normal
and someone said it was
very moving.
Well, well.

This remembering.

I can't forget, shall not forget, your fate.
The purple face and the
orange shirt as you died
or the little limp body bundled in
the ambulance men's arms,

or the amazing chiselled white
face with the ludicrous pie frill
in the coffin
and a little lurking, quirkish
smile, so still,
so unreachable.

Or, most vivid of all, earlier,
the stumbling figure,
all arms, legs and a grey face

searching for comfort
that came home to me
for the last time.

Dido didn't know what she was asking;
The fate is what one remembers.
It is harder to forget that
than the real, funny, warm,
jesting, collapsible, firm,
tight-rope-walking
aerobatic
topsy-turvy
inconceivable, amazing, true
Denis I knew.
All that richness I cannot now capture and hold.

Lesson

Rain is outside.
Grief, or something they give that name,
is somewhere inside
not very far away.
Tears already this morning
then thank God a joke
and the sky lifted
momentarily.

I have explained something to the class,
with care to be precise, and if possible helpful.
Criticism, I explain, is like the surgeon's knife
that probes the source of disturbance.
Appreciation
is love. I do not tell them
that it is love that runs out, runs out
to meet its beloved.
They must learn accuracy first. They are boys.

There is silence now, warmth,
a gentle creaking of chairs,
desks,
someone whispering,
something lurking. No fear, however.
They work. At a poem –
'Schoolroom on a wet afternoon'.
The word 'bereaved'
gentle and blank
chooses my eye from the page.

A boy looks up and smiles. He
hides away a paper dart. I smile back.
This often happens.
Nothing is complete in itself. Not even grief.
Not even life. Or death.
Rain is outside.

Radar Signal

Smooth and amazing speed
out of Euston and on
to the North.

Children's chatter;
The white lion at Whipsnade;
Rupert Bear.
A man reading "Death's Head" –
A mother an Agatha Christie.
An elderly Englishman with a friendly face
gives a lecture on radar
to an eager Pakistani.

Coffee. The sky dulling.
Huge kilns against a red sun.
Lights come on
at Stoke-on-Trent.
Mild interest in an S. F. story,
stiffness, boredom.
The train glides on.

I reach in my bag for a diary
hoping for a map of England
to tell me where Stoke-on-Trent is.
No map. Diaries are not
what they used to be. On we go
and nowhere deepens about us.

A page in the diary lists
abbreviations commonly used –
R.I.P. suddenly leaps out:
Requiescat in pace.

And then, in your firm writing
and your voice.
'*R.S.V.P. – répondez s'il vous plait.*'

Yes, my love. I love you. Rest in Peace.

Cobblestones

We rode through autumn dusk
and back through dark,
Now is the winter –

but I'm not discontented exactly.
It was a good meal.
There were many comforting things –
a tortoise-shaped bell
in the fireplace
(you, and your music),
a brass lizard looking very like you.
Lizards flick about – grin – bask in the sun.
I drank a whisky,
lighted everyone's cigarettes
with your lighter
which goes everywhere with me now
like a small square comforting worry-bead.

(The music played quietly
'Smile when your heart is breaking'
I searched for the name Noël Coward
remembering 'Strange how potent
cheap music is'.
Lucky them, they were together
when he said that)

You seemed to be there,
all the time,
wanting to give us a good party
as you always did.
But we couldn't hear you
or tell you why
there were so many silences;
and I felt you puzzled
and anxious as you hovered and poured wine
and my back ached
and not to be able to see you
really
was a hollowness
bending my back to a hoop
Knowing you were there and longing
for us to be happy.

My mother said today
'What a wonderful summer!
and now this autumn –
all these colours, and so still –
it has been an *Annus Mirabilis*.'

Yes. To be wondered at. The autumn,
                and the year you died.

Machine?

A digger with a long yellow probe
Nuzzles the narrow chalk trench, a mare with a nosebag.
The men stand round, regarding it
With affection.

Research

Today in the gravel pit
Water is calm and mirror-like. A digger,
(Off work for a spell: no clank or splash or scooping –
No moving to be done at all: just peace
To be aware of, and arrested by)
Poised at the water's edge, reflects, enquiring.

'My image in the water
And all this unplumbed depth of clouds, and blue.
No point in scooping for that sky –
That sudden, peaceful sky.
So this is my reflection after all –
Narcissus, I.'

Dignity and Indignation

'They', for horrible reasons best known to themselves,
Have drained my gravel-pit, left my diggers unneeded.
So gaping a hole in the ground is a pitiful thing.
There are a few isolated puddles in the bottom,
    But you can't Dig, in a puddle.

The diggers stand inert, disconsolate.
They turn their backs and gaze across the fields,
Praying perhaps, bitterly, for an act of God –
         An inundation –
Angry and cataclysmic and full to overflowing
With retribution and restoration of justice.

Water Table

One of my diggers is at work again –
   The ponds are filling up
Slowly. Slowly. No inundation.

I am absurdly happy watching it each day
As I drive past, going to work myself.
I wonder if it knows how much fellow-feeling
There is between us, how pleased I am for my digger.
Its back is turned, but I think I can see it grinning.
I grin and grin. It is really quite ridiculous!

Weeds that occupied the new islands during the puddle stage
   Had every intention of staying.
Their brief conquest may have been well-meant
But it's over now. They will soon be flooded again.
And their bodies and seeds, among gravel and mud,
Will make good rich scoop for my digger –
Richer, indeed, than he knows or is bothered about.

What interests him is gravel.
And the river running sweetly through all this valley,
Filtering, filling, seeping and drawing –
   This movement in time and in place
Is his food and his drink, his deity,
   His sense of fulfilment – and space.
And his bucket and chain, lifting, splashing or still,
Mirror him out the peace of his will
   In withholding and grace.

Time Out of Mind (Remembered from Bedlam)

One summer evening they led us out for a while
To watch the morris dancers jigging in style.
We watched, relentlessly; some even forced a smile.
Afterwards the scene was etched on one's mind –
The sunset. The morris dancers and the wind.
Us. The trees. The echoing dark behind.

What kind of meeting was there? Who can tell?
Did they catch sight of our faces before night fell?
One hoped not. They were facing the wind and the light,
And we sat staring beyond them into the night.

Driftwood

They bent me to my task alongside others.
My home was where I creaked and worked,
Straining at nails, not understanding or caring
Though waves crashed and fell back,
Though I rose up the grey sky and fell
Spurning the salt spray – or, hung in a hollow, steadied
To lift again. My tensed purpose also theirs.

Idling in torrid harbours, lipped by greasy swell,
Nosed by nameless shapes, sifted and hosed by rain,
I was patient, I waited to ride again.
Patience was silent purpose.

Out to the darkness once more we ran, hauling together,
Scoured of the scum, seared and whipped with salt.
Roaring dark and wetness bore us down
Down onto rock.

  Shattered, we knew a power
Darker, deeper than wood – the crash, then the silence.
Silence of utter durance, immobility. Rock.
  Inert the nerves now…
  Mindless the quiet now…
  I am a plank.

Water lifts, laps under – the sunlight, aimless,
Above and below lazily flicking and trembling.
I am whetted and rounded, sanded smooth as a pebble.
Lighter than life, I stray and slither and tumble.
Bland as a bone, and bleached, I know the sun
As ultimate opposite now. I blank him back.

Shouldered shoreward I rattle and shelve and settle
On silent shells. Softly the sand receives me,
Holds me between two wave-breaths, yields me again
To the questing, frothy, aimless tongue of the sea;
Then nudges me up again. I am lipped and beached –
My rhythm now the sea, the sand – and the sun.
I lift a blank grey face. So this it is
To be driftwood. To have no plan...
    Eternity begins.

The sun eyes me. Far off, over the sands,
There comes, searching, a Man. Nails in His hands.

Last Lines: New Lines

The boatmen are searing rope ends
      so that they will not fray.
I must turn now up river and face the wind.
I'm glad I can also find
        the sun that way.

The Scarf and the Mountain

There's a hollow now around this calendar day –
A blank. As this motionless month draws near,
I'm aware that it's coming
And that normally I'd be doing
   something to celebrate
   this day. Your birthday.

But two winters now since you died
I've mentally shopped for the CDs you might like
The bright, warm, woolly gloves, scarf, hat
The pretty vase to hold the flowers you loved
Or a book – gripping or funny –
To take your mind off the cancer
That somehow never managed to douse your wit
Your sense of fun.

Only, just sometimes, during a chat on the phone
There'd be a pause. Detachment.
Silence.
And I'd sense your mind shifting
To some bleak, bare mountain-side of attention
That underlay your laughter,
Called for all your courage –
Not to be denied or cajoled away.
Not to be spoken.

What can the warmest woolly scarf do?
The years must go by now
And the date be coming and gone
Covered over by other dates and days –
Phone calls, plans, paraphernalia of living.

Perhaps the scarf was something after all.
Once you said 'Words are all we have'.
But of the bare mountain, most of us have no words.
My words were a warm scarf
For the protection of you –
My little sister whom I loved.

It was very near the end, near the bare mountain,
You handed the scarf and the gloves
To someone you loved who needed them more.

That makes me glad –
In case my own mountain might be cold and near.
And might have to be faced
    without scarf or gloves.

APPENDIX

Cathy

Someone has died, achieving this,
As far as I'm concerned, with almost total
anonymity.

But the trees and the winter fields told me of loss.
Where the contented stream in summer threads
The valley willow-banked, there was an emptiness
Of something more than just the leaves.

And the slow flight of the birds, the lowered sky,
Warned me of sorrow.

Hungry for facts I glean a few: she died
It seems, in spring. Her body lies
In jonquil-gleaming grass beside the sea
In Wales. Around her, primroses
Sprawl wild in April.

I do not know her age – a mother misses her,
She might be child or woman – but I know
She bore pain bravely and her end came soon,
Leaving it seems, a spreading ring
Of loneliness in the dark waters to mark
Her passing.

Strange that I should not recognise you, Cathy,
If we were now to meet; should not exchange
More than a casual, friendly, look and smile,
Missing the person that you are to me, now gone,
Now I shall never meet you as a friend.

For ever now the willow, tree of sorrow
And Ophelia dead must bear new meaning.
Flower-soaked elegies must ineluctably
Recall your going and your poet's pain,
Calling to me across the winter fields, the spring
And summer riches – this flower-strewn world.
Ophelia, willow, willow, Cathy, rue.
But chiefly now it's rosemary, remembrance,
Friend whom I never knew.

Autumn/Winter 1966

On reading a poem by Juliet Gowan (published in The Critical
Quarterly*), mourning the death of her friend. Juliet and I had not, at
this time, met; though later we became close friends.*

April O'Leary

NOTES

For Geoffrey Chaucer Chaucer's adoration of the daisy can be found in the *Prologue to the Legend of Good Women*. (There he describes himself as being pretty stout – and the whole scene is fresh and delightful.) Chaucer was 'Clerk of the Works' to John O'Gaunt. Not many 'great clerks' of Eng. Lit. could say the same!

In Defence of Not putting my Poems into any Order other than Chronological In the Lake District, 'meadow' is a relative term, since these meadows are quite high up and sloping, with exposed rock surfaces.

Churchyard This is the first of the four 'Cathy' poems, the others being *Cathy: Oxford, How Should I Your True-love Know?* and *Landscape with Snow*.
'hospital' – Warneford Hospital in Oxford; 'canal' – small cut in The Parks; 'little church' – Aberaeron, Wales.

Cathy: Oxford I met Cathy in the Warneford Hospital, Oxford, and we were friends (on the basis of shared experiences of teaching and of illness) for the short remainder of her life. Cathy was not really a cynic – her descriptions of teaching in infant school were hilarious and heart-warming. She claimed medication had 'pickled' her – she had applied for over 20 jobs whenever she was 'better' but no one would give her the break she needed so desperately. Her life story had begun just before the fall of Singapore (1942), when her father went missing and her mother walked her (a small child) to Australia and then home. Despite this early trauma, she only succumbed finally to illness while in her second year at Somerville College, Oxford. She was very bright and great fun to be with, even in the spells of gloom.

These poems were written in the spring, summer, autumn and winter following Cathy's death. Sister April O'Leary read them in *The Critical Quarterly* (and *Critical Survey*) long before she and I ever met – and responded with the lovely poem printed in the Appendix to this volume, which she addressed to 'friend whom I never knew', meaning Cathy herself. A few years after that, April and I did meet, accidentally, and became firm friends. Though sheer geography has been against us, astonishing chances have kept bringing us back in touch. This poem of April's is not her only one: she is a sensitive and accomplished poet and has written much lovely work besides this one, which I gratefully print here.

'How Should I Your True-love Know?' Stratford – an amazing production of *Hamlet*. The title comes, of course, from Ophelia's 'mad' song about her father. One of those times when you think grief has faded, but suddenly it leaps up and hits you.

Landscape with Snow The old road from Oxford to Eton. Stokenchurch, probably. My first poem to be published. It won second prize (£5, no less!) in *The Critical Survey* Poetry Competition in 1964.

Psst! Here's the Key. The Gang's Waiting! Parking meters had just been installed in Malet Street in London and their surrounds were left, for a while, unconcreted.

'...Destiny, that hath to instrument this lower world...' Written after teaching at an evening class. (I had a kipper in my pocket). Title taken from *The Tempest*.

New Estate Written when I was in my early twenties and working in Slough.

Covenant Twickenham was where, perhaps, I first became aware of the magic of chestnut trees, and started to explore.

'Oure Hooste' The fruit of the horse chestnut is inedible (obviously): the sweet chestnut, which offers a marvellous feast, should be envisaged here.

Seeing and Catching This is the fourth in the group of 'Chestnut Tree' poems. It is made up of glimpses at Eton, Winchester, Twickenham. The other poems in the group are *Covenant*, *God's Language* and *'Oure Hooste'*.

Convalescent Written after a long bout of flu, in the winter of 1949, at Downe House School. I was diagnosed last and was last in the convalescent bedroom.

Trouble in Mind Title taken from an American blues song: 'Trouble in mind, I'm blue/But I won't be blue always…'.

Dies Irae: Slug in the Wet Wood Cottage, Lake District. Everything was slate there – and rain of course.

Spring-Fall Memory from Warneford Hospital, Oxford. My doctor found me trying to swing on a branch.

Poets Yorkshire Dales. Memory of bathing in the water of a hill-stream, known as a 'beck', when I was eight or nine.

Involvement An evening in Eton – from a high window near Barnes Pool.

Plastic Surgery I wrote this at a time – in the late 1960s – when a new and dreadful bus was brought out in London. It didn't last and I have no quarrel with the present fleet which *is* friendly (though once I did put my foot out and the bus stood on it).

'Nous n'irons plus aux bois...' Lake District. An incredibly late spring, bitterly cold and grey. It must have been *late* May when I wrote this.

Hot London. Someone told me this was a poem about sex. Well, well! I was, simply, terribly hot.

Ache 'Grey window' was in the Common Room of Sidney Webb College, London, where I was a lecturer for a time.

Pilgrimage of Princes This poem was written on a piece of A4 paper that had the words '*Pilgrimage of Princes*' already at the top. This was the title of one of the books owned and read by Edward Pudsey in the sixteenth century: his *Commonplace Book* was the subject of my M.Phil research, 1967. I left the title there, as it seemed to fit my poem.

Snow in March Birmingham, about 1982. A little branch line with clean, modern stations had just been opened to run through Birmingham University and out to Sutton Coldfield. This all happened, as precisely as I could capture it, at the station called 'University', which is perched quite high amid trees.

Selfhood This title was suggested by my first husband, Denis Garland (who died in 1973). I had not given it a title, but he was quite definite. The poem is, of course, about very early cloning experiments, so I sent it recently to the Human Genetics people. They did not reply.

The Gentle Rain: A Villanelle Written in a classroom overlooking tall fir trees, as an English exercise at Downe House School, near Newbury, where I was a pupil. We were studying a lovely book called *English Lyrical Types* and had reached the villanelle. This kind of poem has rules which I don't always follow to the letter. I do hope to catch the spirit, though.

The Violin Tries to Understand False Relation   Again from a high window at Eton. It was a strange climbing pear tree that straggled up to the third storey.

Two Library Ghosts   Working in the Old North Library of the British Museum during the final period of my research, I met a large and impressive American scholar called Seth, who was working for a year on Shakespeare's imagery in *Othello*. I seem to have fallen deeply in love with this genial, neurotic, grizzle-headed person. I took him on outings to Stratford and Windsor, and gave him tomato soup on Hampstead Heath. At last he wrote me a valedictory letter in which, it appeared, I was Ariel (to his Prospero?) and should 'go free'. He wanted to, anyway, so I was heartbroken – hence the many poems about him, written over a long period. The others are *Ache, Loving and Wrecking, The Violin Tries to Understand False Relation, Battering Rams, Dominant, Currency, Recognition I and II, Two Songs: One, Song for Aucassin and Nicolette*.

Bedsocks   Remembered from a chance encounter at a *Critical Quarterly* conference. *The Critical Quarterly* was, in a sense, my university – since both the degrees I did were really 'external'. Brian Cox and Tony Dyson provided the intellectual stimulus and critical zest which is lacking if you're working alone. I know full well how much I owe them.

Incommunicado Eton playing fields, known to me as an infant and later as a 'carer' of infants.

The Old Ladies A composite portrait of a) my maternal grandmother; b) my paternal grandmother (ex-Indian Civil Service); and c) Connie, whom I used to visit in Winchester, because the lady who cleaned our rooms lived with her rent free, as 'carer'.

'Briar Rose' The subheading explains this, but it was a news headline, announcing what may well have been the first instance of what is now quite common.

Battering Rams Windsor Castle.

Currency When I offered this poem to *The Economist*, the then editor replied, charmingly, that he thought it 'elegant' but that poetry was 'a field in which *The Economist*, as such, would not dare to tread'.

Aplomb 'advances *it* dignity' *is* what I meant, because this is seen as a kind of banking 'advance' – denoting adulthood conferred on a small tree by a big bird.

An April Affair London. Teaching at Sidney Webb College. The hail and the petals happened, near the Wallace Museum.

On the Other Side The suburbs of Slough, very neat and sweet. A 'tight little lady' names her house in keeping with the kind of Christmas card that has ladies in crinolines stepping daintily to a stage-y church. My heart bled for the sad Town Clerk, wistfully naming the road. Then I saw the torn picture in a puddle.

In the Land of the Parliaments   Cardinal Mindszenty.

Travelling North   Written on Alnmouth station, on a white paper bag – nothing else available – with one sheep-dog looking on. I meant to go to Edinburgh, but got off on impulse.

Longing   At the funeral service for my sister, Button (Cecilia), held on 3rd August 2001, her family chose this poem to be read out by her daughter, Katy Bingham.

Late Christening   On recovering from a breakdown.

Knutsford Service Centre   the word 'kingly' glances at the King Canute (Knut) who knew (contrary to popular belief) that he could not stem the tide. He was 'condemned' to motion/'progress' just as we are.

Crazy Bird   This is the first of the five 'Denis' poems, the others being *'Remember me! But ah, forget my fate!'*, *Lesson*, *Radar Signal* and *Cobblestones*. To me, Denis was my first, and definite, husband – the word 'partner' is not adequate. He was delightful and difficult, funny and musical. His sudden death at 56, from a heart attack, while sitting right next to me, was an appalling blow: I had reckoned to be devotedly getting him raw-egg-in-coffee for breakfast for another 20 years or more.

   I went on teaching, at Rutlish School, Merton, for a time. The train journeys recorded here were to Manchester (home of my beloved sister, Button) and the Lake District, where my parents by then lived.

Lesson   Rutlish School, Merton. A lesson in the annexe, evening (probably November).

Cobblestones 'Cobblestones' was the name of a rather up-market restaurant in the southern Lake District. My parents and I had gone there 'to cheer me up'.

Machine? This is the first of the four 'Digger' poems, the others being *Research, Dignity and Indignation* and *Water Table*. The latter three poems describe the crane-like, bucket-and-chain-type diggers I watched from the M4 on journeys from Eton to the British Museum where I was studying. The digger described in *Machine?* was different – a tough trench worker seen in Winchester at an earlier date. It is no effort for me to see them as human, and to write about their feelings. They are, after all, vital extensions of the human arm and hands.

Time Out of Mind 'Bedlam' signifies (in this case) the Warneford Hospital, Oxford. I was on a locked ward for six months.

Driftwood John Wain liked this. He heard me read it in Oxford once, and kindly said it was 'a fine sea poem'. But when I first wrote it at the end of a spell in the Warneford, I taped up the book and vowed never to read it again – its world seemed too bleak and lost to contemplate.

Last Lines: New Lines London. The Thames, where I fled on foot from the British Museum after Seth 'ditched' me. I sat writing on the quayside and as I got up to go, one of the boatmen called up cheerily 'Got your poem all right, miss?' and I said 'Yes, thanks!'

PUBLICATION CREDITS

Loving and Wrecking: Spring Storm appeared in *The Spectator* on 21 October 2000 (under the name Juliet Rees).

Churchyard, Cathy: Oxford and *How Should I Your True-love Know?* all originally appeared in *The Critical Quarterly*, Vol. 8, No. 3, autumn 1966.

Landscape with Snow originally appeared in *The Critical Survey*, Vol. 2, No. 1, winter 1964 under the title *Cathy*.

This City Now originally appeared in *The Critical Quarterly*, Vol. 13, No. 3, autumn 1971 and in *The Critical Quarterly* volume *Best Poems of 1971.*

Covenant, God's Language, 'Oure Hooste' and *Seeing and Catching* all originally appeared in *The Critical Quarterly*, Vol. 9, No. 2, summer 1967.

Ache appeared as a frontispiece in Jessica Rees's autobiography: *Sing a Song of Silence* (Kensal Press, 1983).

Nous n'irons plus aux bois and *Time Out of Mind (Remembered from Bedlam)* originally appeared in *The Critical Quarterly*, Vol. 12, No. 4, winter 1970.

Lesson also appeared in *Oxford Originals: An Anthology of Writing from Lady Margaret Hall, 1879–2001*, edited by Stacy Marking (Lady Margaret Hall, 2001).

Driftwood originally appeared in the magazine *Outposts* (ed. H. Sarjeant) in the early 1970s. The exact date and issue number cannot be traced owing to the inaccessibility of records.